First published in Great Britain in 2016 by JBK Books

Text & Illustrations©Jazmin Begum Kennedy

Illustrations: www.colorsandtunes.com

Printed in UK

All rights reserved.

No part of this publication may be reproduced, stored in a retrieval system or transmitted in any form or by any means, electronic, mechanical, photocopying, recording or otherwise, without prior permission of the publisher.

No School Today?

Written By Jazmin Begum Kennedy
& Fatimah-Zahra Kennedy

Published by JBK Books ©2016

Dedication:

We dedicate this book to all the homeschoolers, may we continue to have the strength to educate, enlighten and eradicate the misconceptions that are associated with Home Education.

About the Authors:

Jazmin Begum Kennedy (JBK) is the author of Mercy Like the Raindrops, Blessed Bees and the upcoming novella 15 (Fifteen). She is a retired Teacher, Home Educator, Counsellor and Women's Aid Worker for the charity, The Nisa Foundation.

Fatimah-Zahra Kennedy is JBK's 10 year old Home Educated daughter. She is the author of the book My Granny, which is heart-warming story about the special bond between a little Muslim girl and her Christian grandmother.

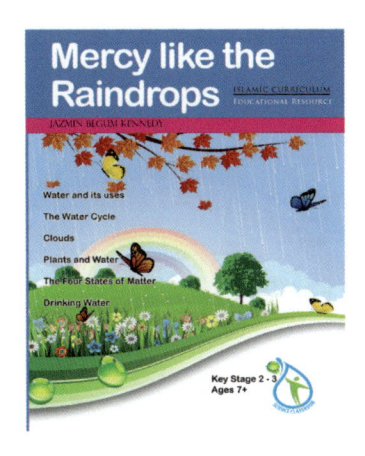

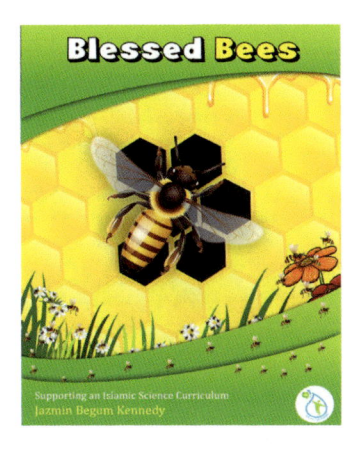

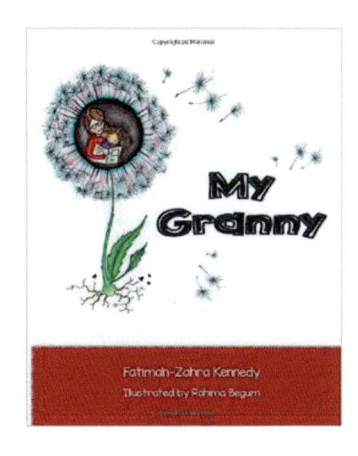

On Monday we went to the dentists and the dentist said, "No school today?"
My mama smiled and my brother replied, "No, we don't go to *school* any day."

The dentist was fascinated and wanted to know more.
I told him about our homeschooling adventures and how we like to explore.

Monday

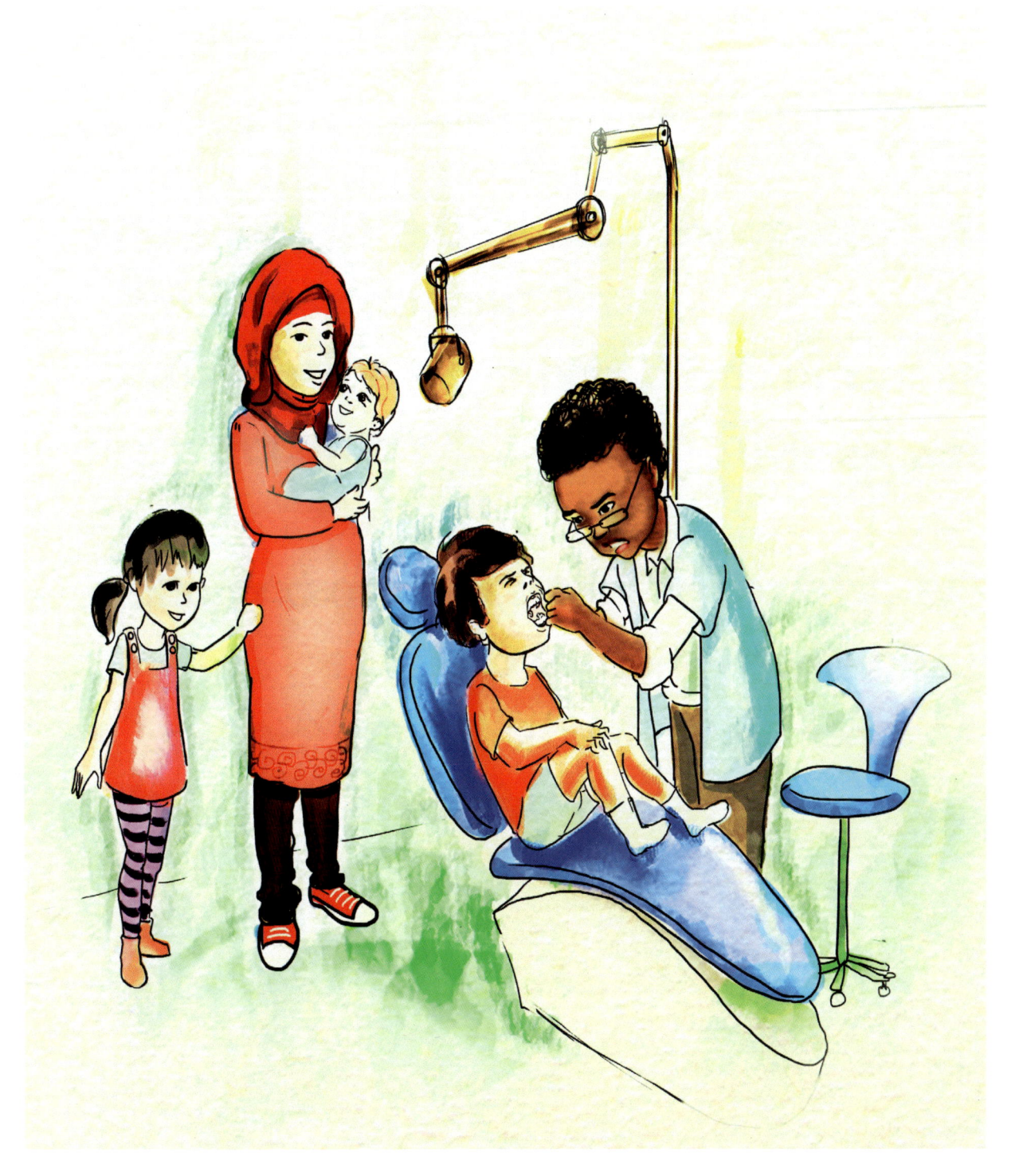

On Tuesday we went to the opticians and the optometrist said, "No school today?" My mama smiled and my brother replied, "No, we don't go to *school* any day."

The optometrist found it interesting and asked what we do all day.
I told her we do Maths, English, Science; we make, we bake and we play.

Tuesday

On Wednesday we went to the supermarket and the cashier said, "No school today?" My mama grinned and my brother exclaimed, "No, we don't go to *school* any day."

The cashier was surprised and asked if not going to school was even allowed.
My mama said, "Yes, of course, we follow the law of the land," she said, sounding proud.

Wednesday

On Thursday we went to the pharmacy and the pharmacist said, "No school today?"
My mama grinned and my brother exclaimed, "No, we don't go to *school* any day."

The pharmacist looked confused, then asked, "What about tests and exams?"
I said, "When we are ready we will sit them, we do have great future plans."

Thursday

On Friday we went to the doctors and the doctor said, "No school today?"
My mama sighed and my brother groaned, "No, we don't go to *school* and we're sick anyway!"

The doctor remembered who we were and said, "Oh, you're still home educated?"
I said, "Of course doctor, we are very dedicated!"

Friday

On Saturday we went to the park and another mum said, "Are you enjoying the school holidays?"

My mama smiled and my brother replied, "It's Saturday and we don't go to *school anyways!*"

The mum was shocked, she said, "No school, who teaches you then?"

I said, "My mama of course, she taught us to read, write and count beyond 10!"

Saturday

On Sunday, we went to a restaurant and the waiter said, "Going back to school tomorrow?"
My mama sighed and my brother replied, "Yes, to our *school* in Kilimanjaro! "

We had a little giggle and then gave out a sigh,
Monday will bring the same questions, I wonder, what would you reply?

Sunday

Questions & Answers

(about homeschooling, taken from the article 'So You Want to Homechool?' by JBK)

Is it legal?

One of the biggest misconceptions about homeschooling is that it's illegal and all the people who are home educating are breaking some kind of law of the land. This is completely incorrect! In England and Wales, home education is given equal status with schools under Section 7 of the Education Act 1996 which clearly states:

'The parent of every child of compulsory school age shall cause him to receive efficient full time education suitable a) to his age ability and aptitude, and b) any special educational needs he may have, either by attendance at a school or otherwise.'

Where "otherwise" actually refers to the right to home educate your child.

I love this quote by George Santayana:

"A child educated only at school is an uneducated child."

So don't worry about getting arrested; focus on how you're going to fit everything in. That's the problem most homeschoolers have; there just isn't enough hours in the day for us!

Do I have to be a Qualified Teacher or have a Degree in certain subjects to Home Educate?

Most definitely not! This is another huge misconception that people have; most insist that you have to be a teacher to homeschool.

Ask yourself, who taught your children to crawl, walk, eat and talk? Did you send them to school to be weaned, potty trained or sleep through the night? These are very difficult things to do and a lot of qualified teachers would not have experienced any of the 'hardship's that we have faced when our children were younger. But we did; they are walking, talking, pooping and eating and there was no need to send them to an institution to master it all. It was us who did it, we were their first teachers.

Everything has been created with an instinct to learn and to imitate so the best qualification we really need is to be the greatest role models for our children. If we can master that then we have succeeded.

Educating a child is a natural process. Homeschooling is nothing more than an extension of parenting.
(Sue Maakestad)

Do I need to follow the National Curriculum or anything specific?

Nope. It is up to you what you want to teach your children so teach according to their interest. Although, there is no harm in looking at different curriculums to get an idea, especially if you are pro-structure (not everyone is). My advice is not to rely heavily on something because if you can't follow it to a T then you will feel like a failure. Take the good and leave the unnecessary stuff behind.

Once you find out your children's learning curb, for example if they are visual, auditory or kinaesthetic learners, you can then plan for the right education that is suited to them.

Print, laminate and hang this quote:

Tell me and I forget. Teach me and I remember. Involve me and I learn. (Benjamin Franklin)

I have a simple topic based curriculum which is cross curricular. For example, if my children *choose* the topic Human Body, then we link it to History. We look at various illnesses that affected people in the past, what medicine was available and who invented it. For Islamic Studies, we would discuss what illnesses is mentioned in the Quran and if a cure is mentioned. For Geography, we would explore the statistics of the illness in other countries etc. The possibilities are endless.

We also do a lot of Lapbooks and Notebooking. A Lapbook is topic based project where children use various mini books to fill in the information. This is a great way of learning about a particular topic with little chunks of writing. www.homeschoolshare.com has 100s of free lapbooks, it's one of our favourite sites.

Notebooking is more suitable for older children, it involves a lot of writing but is a great way of working on a project. My favourite Notebooking pages come from Imans Homeschool, she has a lot of other great resources too. www.imanshomeschool.wordpress.com

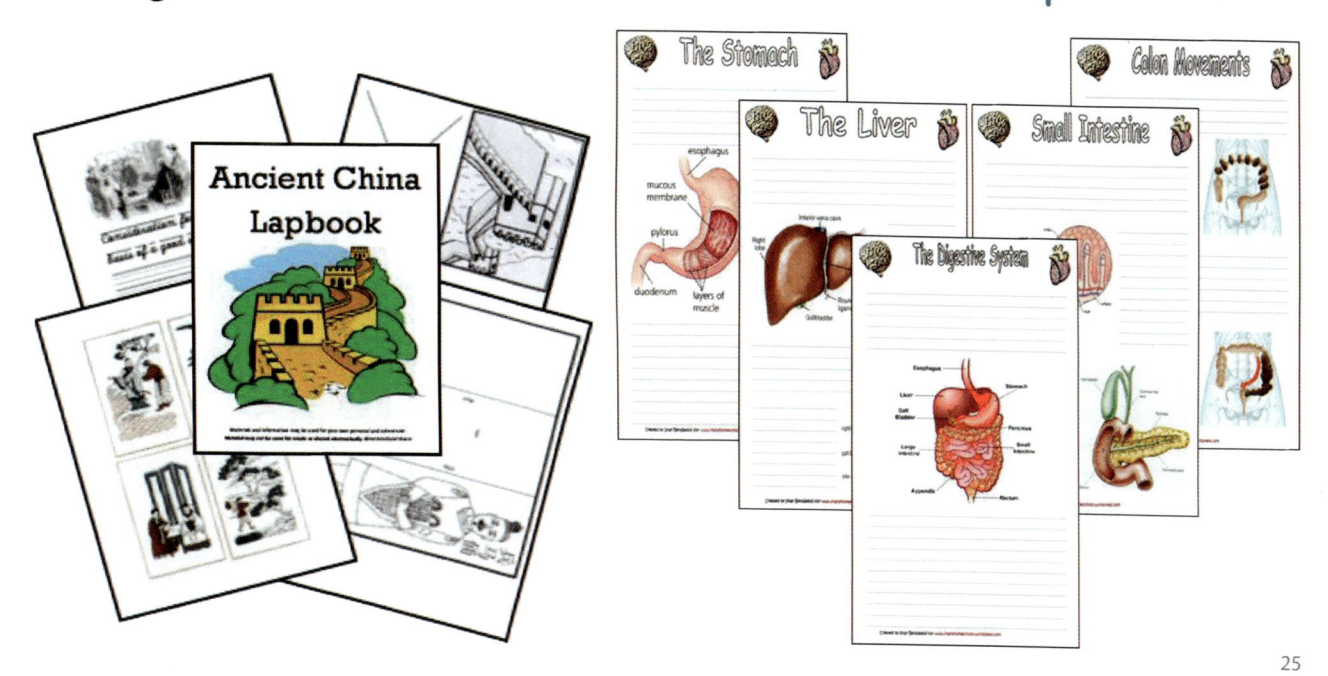

Is it expensive?

To be honest, it's how expensive you make it. The most essential thing you will need for homeschooling is books, books and more books! Use the libraries to your advantage and then gradually build up a home library. Books aren't expensive but the information they contain are priceless. Go to your local carboot sale, you will pick up some great reads for pennies. Make sure you have a vast selection of fiction and non-fiction books readily available. Introduce your children to different genres and cultures, let them develop a thirst for reading and ultimately learning.

The Book People are amazing! You can pick up whole sets for a great price. www.thebookpeople.co.uk.

Educational resources are widely available and they are inexpensive. Be creative and make your own by recycling everyday materials. Utilise Google, Pinterest and Youtube. If you are on Facebook then join all the highly informative homeschooling pages and jot down ideas. There is a wealth of information out there, take some time out and bookmark them. Knowledge is power.

I run the Greater Manchester Home Educators Facebook group. You can find an extensive list of online resources amongst many other helpful tips there. Also, The Resource Lady on Facebook sell great, affordable homeschooling resources and is run by fellow homeschooling mothers.

Another site run by a homeschooling mama is Karimah's Crafts: www.karimascrafts.com You can find brilliant step by step craft projects on there.

Our favourite site for worksheets is superteacherworksheets. Although we do a lot of hands on activities and lapbooks, we also use this site a lot. It is the only site that we actually pay for. At $19.95 per year, you do get your money's worth. There are several comprehensions which coincides with common topics studied and lots of mathematical concepts explained in a fun way. We also love the free sites, worksheetfun.com and myteachingstation.com

If your children learn best through textbooks then Galore Park books are highly recommended. We use the Science, History and Geography for independent learning. The best reading books for Maths, Science, History and Geography are the Horrible Series. They are factual, quirky (sometimes silly!) and very interesting.

Do I need to set up a classroom?

The answer to this question is NO, nope, nay!
It's not a requirement that you try to recreate a classroom setting in your home. The whole world is a classroom, from the home, to the park, libraries and even the shops. Utilise it all.

"When you homeschool, the world is your classroom"

However, many people do have amazing classrooms/study areas and that's perfectly fine as well, it all depends on the needs of your family. I have seen some fabulous study rooms, fully kitted with whiteboards, display boards and quirky storage to drool over.

Before my children turned 7, they did most activities on the floor but once they started formal learning, I realised we needed a table and chairs to improve their writing skills. Due to this, we have a fully equipped room that holds all our learning materials.

For those who do not have an extra room, my advice is to buy a good storage cupboard that can house everything. I find that a little bit of organisation saves a lot of time in the long run.

But what about 'Socialising?'

Oh the dreaded 'S' word! It is a fact that homeschooled kids are actually more socialised by not being restricted to just their peers. They play with children from all walks of life, ages and even with their siblings. Think about your own schooling. Were you in the same class/year as your brother or sister? Did you meet up at playtime to have a chat? Or was it 'embarrassing' for your older sibling to recognise your existence?

At home, your children could be best friends but in school it's simply understood that they are in a different world. This is how conflicts arise. Our children aren't segregated because of age/ability and there is no assumption that they should have different friend groups that don't include each other.

Yes, children in school socialise but they are restricted to a set time and group. You will not find an entire class of 30+ children playing together; everyone splits up according to popularity and even ability.

We are trying to think outside of the box as our children enjoy spending time together rather than be separated by the 'social norm,' as well as socialising with various members of their wider community.

Will I be hindering my children's confidence?

Confidence really depends on individual personalities. Think about some of the adults you know, they have been through the school system and yet lack confidence in many fields right? There is no research proving that schools actually develop confidence.
Look at assemblies and school plays, not all children participate in them, only the confident children take part.

If school was the only place promoting confidence then there would be no bullying right? Homeschooled children are saved from being ridiculed because of how they dress, how they speak, or because they're not following the current trend. There's no peer pressure or teasing to conform to the 'norm' that is dictated to them.

Also look up famous homeschoolers, you'll be shocked that the likes of Beatrix Potter, C.S Lewis, Albert Einstein, Leonardo da Vinci, Thomas Edison and many, many more were all home educated. The lives of these people are imprinted in our education system and widely studied, yet no one cares about their confidence or if they were socialised!

"Personality and socialization aren't the same thing."
(Steven Pinker)

What if I can't teach 9am-3.30pm?

Don't worry, there is no set time for teaching or learning. Remember you are not recreating school at home. The beauty of homeschooling is that you can take it at your children's pace. If they get frustrated or even bored with something then you can always come back to it.

From experiences of teaching in primary schools, all you need is a maximum of 2 hours a day to cover most topics and that's even after taking breaks in between. The rest of the day can be used to learn through structured play and exploration.

Keep in mind, we don't have registrations, assemblies and lining up to go from A-B. We also don't have 30+ children who need our constant explanation and supervision or holding back the class due to disruption. The great thing about homeschooling is that it's not the end of the world if something doesn't get finished as it won't impact the children's SATS results because they don't sit them!

Follow the mantra that there is always tomorrow to try different methods in explaining something that was not understood today.

What if it all gets too much?

Communication is key and ultimately to ask for help before throwing in the towel. Contrary to belief, home educating does not give you superpowers! There is no shame in asking for help from other homeschooling families, online groups or even the LEA.

If you can afford tutors for subjects you don't feel confident in teaching, then hire them, don't think you're a failure. In secondary schools, different teachers teach different subjects. You won't find one teacher who teaches everything, so why do you have to be a martyr? Even primary aged children have tutors because the teacher just cannot give 30+ children the time they need, so parents are forced to supplement their learning at home.

I strongly believe that it is imperative homeschooling families meet up with other families, either for support or a general chit chat. We all have good and bad days BUT nothing works better than making a prayer and sitting down with a fellow homeschooler, with a cuppa to discuss the highs and lows of the day. (Whilst the kids **"SOCIALISE"** of course.)

Good luck!

Printed in Great Britain
by Amazon